THERE ARE NO SOLID GOLD DANCERS ANYMORE

Adrienne Weiss

There Are No Solid Gold Dancers Anymore

A Junction Book

NIGHTWOOD EDITIONS
2014

Nightwood Editions
P.O. Box 1779
Gibsons, BC VON 1VO
Canada
www.nightwoodeditions.com

TYPOGRAPHY & COVER DESIGN: Carleton Wilson

Nightwood Editions acknowledges financial support from the Government of Canada through the Canada Book Fund and the Canada Council for the Arts, and from the Province of British Columbia through the British Columbia Arts Council and the Book Publisher's Tax Credit.

This book has been produced on 100% post-consumer recycled, ancient-forest-free paper, processed chlorine-free and printed with vegetable-based dyes.

Printed and bound in Canada.

LIBRARY AND ARCHIVES CANADA CATALOGUING IN PUBLICATION

Weiss, Adrienne, 1973-, author
There are no Solid gold dancers anymore / Adrienne Weiss.

Poems.
ISBN 978-0-88971-294-2 (pbk.)

I. Title.

PS8595.E488T44 2014 C811'.54 C2014-900624-1

For Peter

CONTENTS

THE FUTURE COMES ANYWAY

Canadian Girl in Training 13
That Way You Look on Love 14
Mata Hari, Crossing Over 16
The Amazing Criswell 18
Once Upon a Time 20
Fortune's Wheel 26
A Member of the Wait Staff Delivers a Glass of Ice to Oprah 27
The Voice I Want Once Lived in Sausalito 28
The Queen of Voodoo 30
"Untitled," by Zelda Sayre 31
The Future Comes Anyway 32

PRODUCTION 1060

The Tin Man's Take on the Heart 37
The Good Woman's Choice 40
The Witch's Motivation 41
Surrender Dorothy 42
The Straw Man 44
The Man Behind the Curtain 46
The Lion's Courage 47

THE SMALL PART OF THE UNIVERSE

The End 53
The Blackout 55
The Psychic's Verdict 56
The Midway 57
Consumed 58
The Red Light District 61
There Are No Solid Gold Dancers Anymore 62
The Uncle Who Could Walk on Water 64
The Swine and the Pearl 66
Heads or Tails 67
The Small Part of the Universe 68
Magnificent Things Surely Will Come 70

Notes 73
Acknowledgements 77
About the Author 79

All the world's a stage and most of us are desperately unrehearsed.

—Seán O'Casey

The Future Comes Anyway

CANADIAN GIRL IN TRAINING

In this picture, a congregation of crows
meet in the parking lot across from a
thread of wartime houses—brick
sanctuaries that glow in the blue lamp-
light like horsehair. Inside such a one:
a kitchen table full of longnecks she never
could make disappear. And you, in the chair,
bigger than anyone, forever mad at catching
me at the Roxy, forever saying, *Rien ne*
sortira de tout cela déblayage,
your face outlined in working-class black
and white. In this picture, your eyes total
the CN scars, dead-end jobs that followed.
But you'll always be bigger than anyone, in
any chair, in any city. Even outside this
picture, after she dies and all I can do is
watch you shrink. Even after I leave for good
with that *vilain* for Toronto—and
our A-frame house teeters, a domino.
For now, I stay tucked inside this picture,
searching the planets, aligning you
to Mars, my heart. Stranded with crows.

THAT WAY YOU LOOK ON LOVE

After Diana, Princess of Wales

The world has yet to preserve you like a bust,
out of stone and milky marble, as part of a
permanent collection, in a corner of museum
in some cosmopolitan centre, where I could visit
you every Sunday, imagine you, the young adventurer
who wants to kiss a boy in every city; or, the lover
who gypsies to Milan, Paris, Florence with intent,
not fortune in the cards, who calls all encounters
along the way *affairs,* both tumultuous and fleeting.
The world, in turn calls you *fickle,* and you are
like Titania that way, that way you look on love. And
on those Sunday visits, I could study your face's contours—
you, the artist of the self, whose blood the world
expects to be blue should it cut you open, whose
voice protests, *No, my body is a sculpture,* chipped
and moulded by discipline, a Cnidian Venus for
this age, consumed with bulimia, exercise, the ideal
form. So, like Praxiteles, you carve animated ear-
lobes, a lick of hair to embellish brow, a flirtatious
lower lip muscle, and everything you tell yourself
in pursuit of this form, that is your sacrifice and duty,
you believe will come to manifest in reflections in
the glass, all those hungry spectator eyes. And
after all those Sunday visits, I might know enough
to write essays delineating, challenging your importance,
place, in some context of art, all while the world
poses stupidly beside you, holds you up to a still-
impossible standard. Or I might learn after seeing
you stuck, shellacked in a necklace of clavicle,

where the limits of neck perpetually decapitate you,
to hold you beyond any critical gaze, to shun the books,
spent terminologies and years of obsessive scrutiny,
as you face me, the world, as you intended: with eyes
that look no other way but to love.

MATA HARI, CROSSING OVER

Harlot, yes! But traitoress, never!
—Mata Hari, supposedly during her trial for espionage, 1917

I often said I would take Death if
he could pay, and when he failed
to please me, be expected to plea bargain,
add the necessary gratuity. Now with
anticipation, I wait in my cell—a
variation on hell—for his cocked
illumination. Lovers watched as I danced
after him, each susurrated in fictitious exotica,
my excellent lies. Their drawings, either
salacious or full of Egyptian veneration,
made myths of me. But I was more alive
than charcoal or famous *baiseuse*
consummating a reputation. And out of that past
life is a green field, away from the Paris
that still rents me out. Mere days ahead,
he soldiers, in Belgium perhaps. Like him,
I have challenged Luck, been its conqueror;
but now, Luck conquers me, for he is coming,
and when he comes, I will march to him,
love's infidel. I will not haggle or curse
or cross him at the nadir. No, when he
comes to that green field, I will be ready,
and wear my best stockings. I will not turn
my eyes upward, for Death is close to a true
lover as I shall know; I will stand and face him,
quaver under the barrage of kisses, and all

those teeth, baring down, point blank, in
aim of the ultimate peak: my steeled heart.

THE AMAZING CRISWELL

This morning I feel off. Water seduces
me in the shower—Lord help me—
and my hair will not improvise. Even dead,
I stay convincingly restored, despite my
grey pallor, lack of appetite. See, I died
in '82 of cardiac arrest, not my design.
I would have hired muscular acolytes to
overdose on their glamour. Long have I wished
I survived to '85—Jeanne Dixon's walk-
on part on Episode 13 of *Golden Girls*?
So contrived. My words to Rose, a sweeter
dose of reason; the right way to end a lack-
lustre season. And if I return, I will star on
Piers Morgan, predict the world's end once
again: mass cannibalism by reality-star
gorgons, *how sublime,* this time in summer,
2099. If he asks, *How do you know?*
Well, I will say, *It's about how far you let*
your mind go. Truth is, lying is the easy
part. I will bray enough to stop the casket
silencing my telegenic telepathy with such
predictions as: *Don't blow a gasket! Lady*
Gaga to be our first female president! Or,
This time next year, a "lost" tribe of dapper
decadence will be discovered inside Earth
at the North Pole! And Piers? He will merely
query the condition of his soul. Yes, if I
return to the sanguine shores of *E Pluribus Unum,*
it will not be as a has-been, but the certain
king of psychic couture, back to tell the

incredible future (certainly, darlings, we
must all have one pipe dream that fits us as
lovingly as a suture). Now back to me, Piers.
Truth is (a truth I failed to tell Bob Barker's
unneutered cats or Johnny Carson), no one
ever truly dies; take me for example. I keep
escaping like a wiz into the glorious galactic
glamour of space where Liberace reigns like
the Medici, and Blanche basks in a lunar-eclipsed
Miami. Truth is, Piers, I will say *anything* to defy
public sedition, its critical, useless *Why?*,
the question that begs to see us B-hags shoved
into *TMZ*'s version of the body bag like mere
sight gags. Just as the stars from *Jersey Shore*
surely form caliginous clusters, face the
internal storm in which they filibuster
formidably, shout into the silence of TV,
reality's drought—*how could you* make
an end of our wicked beauty? *Oh America,*
they will say with gifted eloquence, and a wink,
and a tweet, *what a world,* what a twisted
world this is, that, like a boxer's embrace,
beats us into bloody conceit.

ONCE UPON A TIME

I: *Pygmalion*

Hours before the St. Valentine's dance,
Cathy's hands assemble Jen's profile:
What she wants is a perfect S-curve,
so she tilts Jen's head, twists one hip.
Then she adds a chain with an over-
sized, dangling cross—*Very Madonna,*
she says, pulling it against Jen's throat,
a heavy choker. Cathy steps back,
examines Jen's immobile form,
judges her handiwork's effect. Then,
together they pose in Cathy's sister's
full-length mirror; their bodies below
the tailbone equally nascent.
Now it is time for Jen to sit, to have
her dirty blonde hair curl under iron's
heat, be a golden Vitruvian wave set
in Cathy's grip. Feeling breathless,
Jen dares undo the chain, lets fall
the cross to her chest. *It looks better*
as a choker, comes the obvious
assessment, as Cathy's fingers sculpt
one winglike tuft to tease, then glue
with hairspray. Jen stares into the mirror,
her likeness framed by the curling
edges of loose photographs jammed
into the thin crevice between pine and
glass. She knows these pictures, has
memorized their critical angles and light,

but where she sits she sees herself only
as a suggestion, a rough outline in their
random compositions, and her hand-
writing across the white bottom of
one Polaroid—*Best friends forever*—
a ghost's script. In the mirror's limited
space, she searches her potential faces,
but it is just Cathy's likeness rolling
its eyes. Jen cannot help but flinch when
the iron's mouth pulls up her scalp and
the two Cathys laugh, as Jen, unchanged,
cries, *Ow. You're hurting me.*

II: *The Fairest of Them All*

In the gym's centre, I dance—me, the girl
other girls call *lucky*. My elastic arms stretch
to hold everybody in—everybody but Jen.
I do not know why Jen and I are friends; it
is annoying how much she thinks she knows
herself. In a way I am grateful, for she gives
me her face: shattered with glitter, a mirror
to reflect against mine down the long, haunting
hallways where our blue eyes exchange
variations of shadow, and sometimes, fear.
Now, a quiet chill awakens in me as "Need
You Tonight" starts, a favourite song to lip-synch,
to imagine I am the song's *you*, needed for
a higher purpose. Boys who do not dare ask
me to dance swing from the ropes as programmed
drums beat to the *total eclipse of my heart*;
some girls might say mine is a cold hard thing,
barely alive, even if smoking iron shoes
were placed before me. But a queen's heart is
its own orbit, full of probable stars, of implosions
no one hears. And, as everyone dances, my
arms strangle the air we breathe, our bodies a
bundle of gasping parts I contain in my grasp
for the length of a hit single or till my arms
snap, release our potential. Only Jen is free, has
an energy I cannot harness. And I wonder what
pressure will break our mirror; whose face will fall
to pieces first, never to be put back together. Even
from so high above I know the hanging boys'
bloodshot eyes linger on me; even in red-hot shoes,

dancing myself to death, I inspire some boys'
stupid devotion, but Jen remains the fairer of us.

III: *The Sea Witch*

Wanting is like choking—and I am a strangled
mouth by the basketball court. Chilly valentines
escape through my teeth. Touching the knee of
the gymnasium's smell with a nail-bitten finger,
I breathe in ten-year-old body odour, the sour note
of watermelon Hubba Bubba. A lonely river of
girl-legs buckle under *Ride your pony! Mony!*
Mony! as Cathy's wicked finger scrutinizes one
girl's submerged body and all the flashy pink fishes
follow that finger like bait, cooing, *Ohmygahd,*
who does she think she is? As if it were embarrassing
to be yourself. As if that girl had not learned her
turn had come, that all she has to do is ride it out
till Zeppelin mournfully erects that stairway,
signalling the end of this terrible dance. I wait
for the end to arrive too, for my mouth to untangle
Cupid's bows, taste words again. But the word is
everyone gets her turn, including the pink fishes who
cower when Cathy nears—each afraid her time is
now, each pitching meagre lace valentines at Cathy's
dreaded, warrior-like feet before slipping back, easily,
into anonymous waters, the girls' washroom, where
they fight tears, flood underwear with toilet paper,
pick 1987 off lips like scabs and inspect tongueless
mouths, the other's fate in the greasy mirror. Some,
like Jen, smack strawberry lip gloss, ingest its waxy
nutrition, while silently conjuring a future as tasty
and long-lasting as watermelon Hubba Bubba.
Cathy beckons me in, but I tell her *Time is up,* turn
my back on its glaring reflection, and exit to the
parking lot where dads wait, headlights glowing

disapproval, where grade elevens huddle behind cars,
exchanging minor revelations in code like a cloud
of mystified magpies. And before closing the
passenger door I hear the glorious, cold words,
happily ever after, gasping for air.

FORTUNE'S WHEEL

Your closest bid leads to a stoned morning—
higher, and you'd have won that stereo system,
not needed a third coffee to awaken the day's
plans, throw open the sun. Outside, a neighbour's
ferocious fake tan blinds the squirrels, and you
believe luck will come when you stumble, will
mean *you deserve it.* You hate Kim and Eric in
Cleveland loves Bob Barker shrouds, graduate
from coffee to Coke, stomach churning to a new
discovery: that you're hardly the type, no, not
like Kim who makes it all the way to Bob's cheek,
Rome's Jacuzzi. No, inside your beautiful, framed
house you wait for a fire to start, while Kim, screaming,
waves from a Mustang convertible and you can't
register that time moves, can shout, *It's already 3*
goddamn 30? Now, John Edward points through
the static at you, regret ticking like the Showcase Wheel.
I'm being told to acknowledge someone out there,
he says, sure to find the dead parts of you, and the
life that still happens there, while you're sure that
Luck, when announced by Rod Roddy, will be
your name, telling you to *Come on down!*

A MEMBER OF THE WAIT STAFF DELIVERS A GLASS OF ICE TO OPRAH

Oh, you're an angel, Oprah said simply when
I rested the glass of ice on the Egyptian linen.
As if I could stretch to sky like a Judas tree,
as if a message was mixed in the lead AH Heisey
wineglass: *the gathering of waters She called seas.*
An entire globe of ocean: plankton, algae, craw-
fish and treasure, an answer swimming in Her maw,
truth's great potion. How beautiful I felt in my
alabaster blouse, my wrinkled slacks and my shy
sensible shoes, to resemble an angel guarding her hull.
And in the glass, I swore I saw Oprah scull
then glide on an improvised raft of sliced lemon,
a knife for an oar.

THE VOICE I WANT ONCE LIVED IN SAUSALITO

Welcome to Paradise, you made it, says
the guy at Sausalito's ferry terminal, and
I believe him, the way the houses perch
perilous in the hilltops, and fathers teach
daughters to fish off velveteen rocks. In
Sausalito, you can get a picture of yourself
holding a white parrot, but we come to
walk Bridgeway in search of a fading white
address, a relic of cultural drift. So we follow
numbers, and I think, what a quixotic pilgrimage
from town, the turbulent sun and breathless
expectation part of the design of things,
as we pass Locust St. unscathed, and the
Lighthouse Coffee Shop provides light sustenance.
The way the air smells it could be February,
1976, and I could be young, and an artist,
desperate to start here where *it is all happening*,
where glamour is a walk in platform boots
off Bridgeway, down a dirt road to Marinship
Way, and into an empty parking lot swathed
by trees with branches that hang like Davy
Jones' bangs. And like a comb's teeth, your
finger points at 2200's oversized font, then
The Record Plant's front door, a carved
menagerie of players playing music as animals,
disciples of sound. I march up to it, rub the
archway's wooden lintel as if a gold lamp,
as if out of splintered grain, a rock n' roll god
waits to grant, in raspy wail, three dreams true:
to come to California, leave it all behind, and

find the voice I want. And I know some dreams
are old and should die, as you take pictures of
the door, but here I am, where it could be 1976,
and like a believer I follow the band through
this February spring, as they arrive at the
beginning of what they cannot yet know, guitars
trailing like second-hand coattails, voices
humming about silver spoons, the front door
inviting the rumours in. In Sausalito, too old now
to live *on the edge of seventeen,* I listen for
the voice I want clamouring to harmony,
caroming off Alcatraz's rock, or dreaming
in Sly's Pit where beautiful lines got drawn
and hearts smashed; I listen for a voice that
wades into its own reverberations, is a familiar
call that pursues, remembers, leads me here,
even if it dissipated into bay air long ago. I stand
at the Plant's front door, as you give names to
the animal players like Johnny Five (frog) and
Jimmy Jive (fox), with the tension of time's
lock at my fingertips, uncertain what my
devotion knows, even when the rain comes
and does not thunder.

THE QUEEN OF VOODOO

I pull out dead strands, I brush, I plait, I smile. I am fast,
take pains not to encourage Mrs. Winslow's dry, flaking scalp.
I twist her thin mane; almost laugh when her mouth opens, and,
like scissors, cuts apart the women she despises: this husband's
absences, that husband's dalliances, all the betrayed confidences.

I catch every falling scrap—patchwork her revelations into complex
tree of life patterns, embroider her secrets with blanket white
stitches. I think about my growing quilt; each square composed
lovingly of discarded truths. Like I said, I am fast.

I apply the pins to keep in place a feathered flourish—she flinches,
though I try hard not to rake her skull. My fingers smart, and I long
for the day I no longer have to serve—when the women come,
begging pardons of me and venerating my words like a saint's.

"UNTITLED," BY ZELDA SAYRE

You have such a beautiful back, it could make
me cry. I want to kiss it all over, but then
I'd wake you, and you'd hate that, as much
as you'd hate your back being kissed, stared
at. A fire is in my belly, I long to say, long to
write, but am afraid how that *sounds* should
I say it out loud; how that *reads* should you
read it and think me silly. I do not want to be
thought of as silly, and do not think myself
this way. My fire a lonely, hungry story I want
you to burn in, simply. But you will not burn
simply for my story. No, you burn to narrate
cities, our bed, the play money that rules our
life. I drag your love behind me—its current
market value—and you write it into stylish
syntax that radiates a green light. My words you
take, mistake for art. Now my hand reaches,
madly, maddeningly close to your skin. But
you do not move, and I am not sure what I love
or hate more: this muscular back, the spine's
crevices and particular strangeness, or your face,
and all its maligned, affected scorn.

THE FUTURE COMES ANYWAY

After Rainer Maria Rilke

We blink, and it is years, not hours
later. Where we sit, the sliding door
sighs, the air reeks of green, and a cool
breeze lies against your throat like
a threat. Those orange lights to the east—
the city you loathe—twinkle with gorgeous
defiance and on the suburban street
where you live, where I used to live,
the houses limp in the darkness. You
blink and turn on the moon like you
turn on the overhead light, arrange your
storybook face, its deepening lines, darker
and darker, till you fall to shadow.
Tonight, where we sit, summer lies
crumpled like a blanket, and the purple
flowers of rampion, spread as wide as
your unrequited love, reach through our
mother's overrun garden, nod to us. You
tell me as you have many times before
that no one knows what it is like to love
the way you do, and I pop a beer can where
words should come in response, where
resignation echoes, slides down my throat,
accommodating the burn of that little
cruelty, which lingers ever still.
In this tumultuous story, where no one
loves her misunderstood prince the way
you do, I skip the pages for a quiet space
to stay still for as long as I can, for tonight,

you insist on stepping into this story's past
because you want me to see its gaping
hollow beauty for myself. So I wait for
the occasional pause, then consider,
in those empty spaces, your old bedroom,
where I will sleep tonight, how it remains pink,
retains our mother's oversized dresser
covered in memory's stain, and stickers
of the galaxy emit a dulled glow on
the ceiling. How there is no finding Earth
where you are .... Now, you indulge in
the story's most recent development, the
prince's lily-livered resurgence, and
wonder if, with each accelerated telling,
each subsequent year you wait for
the dénouement, your heart will burst in
on itself; if you will go further into this
never-ending waiting, each summer
lying like a crumpled blanket, and the
purple flowers of rampion, spread as
wide as your unrequited love, reach through
our mother's overrun garden to nod to
you, only you are older, and have not
learned that the future comes anyway,
your hair a noose bound in its fingers.
I look up. In the sky, on the pink ceiling
upstairs, Mars competes with the Big Dipper,
an uncanny glow. You blink and turn off
the moon, let fall your hair, drift back to
the house, your tower, where I used to live.
For now I stay still, remember there
is morning to come, a city of orange
light to return to, and sip my beer,

wondering what unseen animal plaguing
our mother's overrun garden with
its hunger, will rescue you.

Production 1060

People ask me, "it must have been fun, making that picture… "
Fun? Like hell it was fun! It was a lot of hard work.

—Jack Haley

… In the case of a beloved film, we are all the stars' doubles.…
We are the stand-ins now.

—Salman Rushdie

THE TIN MAN'S TAKE ON THE HEART

I

Some make their living never headlining.
That long void between first and second?
That's what us vaudeville comics used to call,
payin' yer dues, or if we felt nasty, *playin' to*
the haircuts. For some players, the circuit's
like a series of grand juries handcuffed to
the seats. For most of us in this business,
wanting the audience's heart is everything.
But I've learned that expecting to always
have it is another thing. These days, the heart's
in the talkies; and currently, I'm on loan to
MGM from Fox, have inherited Buddy
Ebsen's blistering silver body, its absent heart—
every day, I give every Munchkin, and Victor
Fleming, a fever. And this time around, I may
be second banana to Ebsen, but it's work,
and the money's good. Besides, I've been top
banana at the Palace and Orpheum where
laughs chased me like a litany of heartbeats.

II

Now, despite the silver paste's heat, and
the fifteen-hour days, and my faithfulness
to the part, I cannot pretend to know the
intricacies of anyone's heart. Some say it's as
simple as the old carnie trick of fortune-
telling—a Madame tenderly holding a poor
sap's empty cup, one painted fingernail
pointing into it, and a voice thick with Europe
saying, *See das shape? Vy, das une Kadillac!*
She reads the sap's heart in his natty suit, his
Brylcreemed hair, his rough hands; and
sure enough, he smiles the smile of a hungry
boy in a five and dime with nothing but emptiness
in his pocket—Why the very idea! Me and
such luxury! And whose heart wouldn't want
all that extra, prestigious space if it could
afford the monthly payments? Most, I suppose;
but this heart? It just wants a moment of rest
from its own tired journey in search of itself.

III

One day, as a joke, I peer into Judy's idle tea-
cup and say, *See those shapes? There's a lion*
and tiger and bear all set to fight over love
for you! She laughs her young laugh, *Oh my!*
Yesiree, I continue, as Ray and Bert peer
over the edge of their teacups like two bumbling
Englishmen, *one wrong move shapes every*
banana's future: To go big, pal, or hell,
take the veil. And I guess I've an eye for this
kind of divining: like a ticking time bomb,
the performer's heart the type to forever be
hitched to the fickle stage, yearning for its
shot in the dark, for the rush of the bang-up
finish. Even if such hearts get restless soft-shoe
shufflin' their way through *the merry ol' land*
of Oz, and must gather beneath the hot Klieg
lights to trade Joe Millers between takes. I watch
Judy stare into her cup at the future and
we all laugh as she jokes how I, heartless, must
have hoarded the scum, all her lucky dregs.

THE GOOD WOMAN'S CHOICE

Today's been full: I made crullers, became fearful
for the chicks' health, the other animals *worrying*

themselves into anemia. I prepared, all this time
I suppose, for the cyclone. Could smell it coming

for years. Can smell how it will change things:
the tepid sky, Henry's overcast face, my will.

In this life I made few choices. A good, Christian
woman bears all, her presence an illusion, despite

today's sun stifling my neck; despite Zeke's and
Hickory's and Hunk's jokes; despite the grey mass

coming to suffocate it all. There is much yelling—
horses bay and gallop like fire. Henry pulls me, but

I remember Judy, forever running away; myself, and
what it means to follow now that the credits have rolled.

So I stretch my arms to the unkempt horizon; Henry
gone. A cotton-mouthed Kansas wind lifts me home.

THE WITCH'S MOTIVATION

It is the first take of my disappearing act—
twenty feet off-camera, the star lolls, waiting
for it to be over, yawning into her waiting—
all while MGM's army mobilizes around her bright mouth,
and set designers battle with the giant tendrils of a plastic forest
to better frame her newly dyed crown.
The director's megaphone cannot make her flinch:
After all, the shoes, Margaret, have been stolen from you,
is a direction aimed only at a witch's motivation.
So I advance in my blackened body to the camera, and imagine
I am in my classroom in Rye, New York, and the star is my student.
Her remote voice solves math equations and coos to be excused.
It is clear I am not to like her (this, my motivation), just as it is clear
her dressing room is the one dotted with auspicious gold stars—
such stars reserved for only the best students, to chart and
boast their glorious, public progress. And I, an old girl from
the west, should care little for such vain plotting.
Another take, the director charges, and I fear I will be burned
to my rancorous bone. But I get into position,
to descend into sulphur—the star yawns again—
my ugliness, motivation, so stultifying from so great a divide.

SURRENDER DOROTHY

> *The only mistake I ever made, the only harm I ever did, was sing "Over the Rainbow."*
>
> —Judy Garland to Barbara Walters, 1967

Two minutes, someone calls, and the makeup artist rubs a calloused thumb into the apples of my cheeks. The meticulous imprint of her thumb, ingrained in black powder, now smudges my skin like a fingerprint on a doorknob, like a criminal's mistake.

Isn't it funny someone does this for a living? It's funny that I let her touch me at all. That I don't think twice about such intrusions—the constant plucking and pruning, because, well, you get so used to such things, even if it's all rather nerve-wracking.

Most likely, no one'll notice the smudging's effect, how one touch could so fearlessly embellish a face—its hard lines. And it's hardness I've got, and always had; old, hard me, forever talking to myself in the dark, or standing behind the curtain ready for my encore, in some cases still dressed the tramp, *because there's no time to change,*

Judy, they told me, *you're live.* And don't I know it—a real live wire. So then, as now, I've got to sing that song to a television audience, to a packed Carnegie Hall, no longer That Girl, but a Mother. And a Wife. A Headline. An American Tragedy. And so many other things I haven't yet become.

So the lyrics, they run through my head, like, like the answers to life's big questions. But, you know, I was never like her—I didn't grow up that way. Before she walked that road, I lived like a gypsy child skipping across America's stages for lousy pennies. *Don't you know each cloud contains pennies from heaven .... Pennies ...* to give my mother. Ah, but that's another song, darling, for another time.

I look back at the vanity mirror, contemplate my mouth—should it be redder? Ha—here I am, a tramp with a perfectly red mouth, her heart a perfectly arranged mess of rags. I suppose I was always your tramp, worked to the bone. And I suppose I am, all these years later, still your tramp, still singing for my supper, still singing the same words out of a still perfect and red mouth.

I think about this as I stand facing you all in Carnegie Hall. I think about never singing this song again. That this is it. That this might very well be it. The last goddamn time. And it's like getting off a decades-long train ride, having finally arrived, somewhere, where bluebirds fly, you know? Somewhere like the end, the final surrender.

THE STRAW MAN

I survived it all: Dorchester, vaudeville, the Golden Age,
all those TV variety specials, and yes, Oz. I have front-page
memories of that makeshift and lengthy road I tramped along,
after my hero, the role of my dreams, that perfect song.
I can even now summon the steps I took as, and I quote,
a horse-faced hoofer—the distance I was willing to devote
for a brain. And, by happenstance, the straw man would be
all I would ever need to be; after 1939, no yearly TV or
DVD residuals, just the blessed gift of immortality.
And I am old these days. I have not ruled in Oz for years, and
am unaware of the politics that arose after me. A band
of Winkies took over, perhaps; it was, after all, their time.
Or good ol' Mervyn LeRoy, nestled, all pickled and fat
on a plush throne in Emerald City. Yes, I could see that.
Over time I saw less and less of everyone. A star was born
in Judy, Jack found himself on TV, while Bert was reborn
a savant on Broadway. And back to the grind we were thrust.
We rarely talked of the days we owned that road, or fussed
over the lore that evolved of its own accord. No one but us knew
we sang those tunes as though they were our very due.
Only ten years ago, if I had walked a few blocks down
Beverly Drive, I might have encountered the Tin Man—the man
I did not know how to be—as if we were villagers in Munchkinland.
He lived well, of that I am quite sure, with his heart intact.
I do not know what or if he ever thought of me. In fact,
I survived them all: a good witch and a bad witch, a flying
monkey, a bumbling wizard who knew nothing of wizardry,
a lionhearted terrier and a terrified lion, the lovely girl Dorothy,
or was it Frances or Judy?—I no longer remember which
name her fate later came to curse. Each of us a small, quotidian

part of her legend, like scrap parts from the days of nickelodeon,
when chewing the scenery was a job for the lowly proletarian,
was all the circuit's two-bit players had by way of feeling utopian.
Now I lie in a hospital bed, patient Gwen rubs my forehead.
She talks to comfort me, but I am consultin' with the flowers,
or is it the rain? *Ray,* she calls, and in her eyes are a red
and yellow cornfield where a murder of crows circle a lone, weary
straw man—a ratty obelisk against a rainbow-less sky. I hear
the steps of clicking shoes, the poised bark of a dog, leering
closer—and I am resolved to return, because, as my song knows,
with all the thoughts I must be thinkin', I have much still to learn.

THE MAN BEHIND THE CURTAIN

In a second-hand Prince Albert coat, during a test shot, I suffer
chance: my fingers in one pocket discover, trace over L. Frank Baum's
embroidered initials, and the onus of his vision now follows my
every step and choice, despite that I never walk the yellow brick road.
Not in this picture.

In this temporary city, where I wait for Judy to deliver the goods,
green skyscrapers point needlessly at the studio's sky, could puncture
a synthetic cloud if they tried. Such clouds remind me that in Hollywood
it does not matter what I believe. Yet, in Hollywood, everything depends
on who I believe. So I look up *at clouds that soon will roll me by* and
believe, yesterday in MGM's contract, tomorrow in the mickey of Hayman's
I keep in Baum's velvet-lined pocket, where, perhaps instead, he kept
a money clip, or ideas to sift like change.

Master mind-reader, exhibitionist balloonist, gatekeeper, conman,
cabby, wizard; I am all vocations but no star. It is all I can do to bear
Judy's voice that intimidates love, the big time. It is enough to get
through the Oz sequences and not grimace, or feel the charlatan, with
Baum's philosophy weighing down our pocket. Today I hold my breath,
sneak swigs, pray to make it sane, over the rainbow—wherever
the balloon, like all bad dreams, lands me.

THE LION'S COURAGE

Well, after all, how many lion parts are there?
—Bert Lahr

Always leave them laughing, they said.
Everybody loves a clown, they said. But
the joke ain't everything, kid, and
what's a clown—*ahem,* a lion—
to do these days? Years ago, all I
had to do was *sing about love and*
happy times,
about pretty things,
about plucking strings,
not how life clutches and clings.
Nah, just sing *to give the impression*
we exist, I exist, after Oz. But
life still mistakes me for that lion
galumphing to Arlen and Harburg as
Judy looks into my winking eye, her
gait heavy upon the yellow brick,
and I marvel over her Technicolor head,
fussy hunch of Juliet-sleeves, the
dazzlingly quick tremble of rubied feet,
how with one look I crack her up,
she gives in, and she's mine, kid. That
laugh and all its nerve, mine. I remember
it made a beautiful noise as it fell from
her mouth,
like zayzoozas,
like leaves,

like gnong-gnong-gnong,
like leaves.

Now, as the lion in *Godot,* I am terribly
aware of my jewel-less feet, of not
cracking up Vladimir. My toes gnaw at
relief, blisters spit at joy, and the scabs,
oh, the scabs—
critics'll say I'm a bloody mess messing
up New York's Hollywood Boulevard.
They'll say I splutter like a garden hose. No,
like a fire hydrant,
like an out-of-work fountain,
like a Shakespearean idiot.
All this lousy life I've crawled, dragging
these prideless paws to the stage
where *there's no lack of void* to fill
with whatever's in you, 'cause
all you got is what's in you, kid.

Getting back to my existessential struggle:
There's always one in the front row who
won't laugh at my predicament; always
one who's the elbow in my eye, whose sense
of humour's under construction, who gets
into my subnoxious. But I'm a profesh-ya-nal?
First, a little eye mugging. And if that don't
work, well I could try this. *Ahem.*

ESTRAGON *Is that all there is? I'm going then.* They say absinthe
makes the heart grow fonder.

Wait for it. Wait for the show of teeth—
Ah, nuts. The stage is a cruel place, but crueller
still is silence.
We just need to *have a little courage,*
that's all,
to go on—*Shall we go?*
To let go—*We can't.*
To seize—*Why not?*
One roar—*We're waiting for...*
One little pppfffttt—*I'm waiting for...*
One side-splittin' guffaw—*I'm waiting for...*
How'm ah doin, kid? Tell me
I killed 'em tonight,
that even though they've gone,
they'll *come back to-morrow, and if they come?*
I'll be here waiting
to go on, waiting for
the most beautiful noise to fall from
their mouths,
their eyes,
like zayzoozas,
like leaves,
like gnong-gnong-gnong,
like leaves.

The Small Part of the Universe

THE END

Lunch-break voices blow across city streets,
while the sun, hot as tomato soup, burns our
collective tongue, dilutes our soggy stories.
Horns like trumpet jazz cannot rile hungry office
workers bent over Tupperware like willows,
the glare of untapped dreams popping out of heads
like empty thought bubbles, lingering with exhaust,
waiting for articulation, bursting, soundless. Some
dreams a pulpy mess already years behind us.
We pass the bitter end of a child's need for its
mother, look for a good spot to rest, while the sun
settles atop the city like a collapsed bowler hat.
Today, our sandwiches taste of dying stars, each
bite taking us closer to the end of time, the separate
spaces where we sit and make an inventory of
useless detail, constantly at work to repel the anger
that splits the world's Rumpelstiltskins in two. To
avoid the glare of my co-worker's eyes—like clean
dissection tools—I look west, the sky a tight grey
hose punctured with runs. With her mouth she pulls
me along an assembly line of stories that stretch like
taffy, an aimless swirl to the centre of things where
parents, robed fingertip to elbow in yellow gloves,
disinfect one daughter's messy tongue, its rebel sparks,
while the baby, more worthy of love's protective
power, receives the coveted handkerchief, its three
bloody drops. How I imagine this portrait hanging in
her foyer, those eyes following its perspective past
the front door, certain the reach of line only goes so
far before it intersects with nature, blurs. For now, all

the sun and I can do is cough with polite reservation,
the lunch hour up, while my co-worker retreats into
her portrait's mirror, and I wrap yellow crumbs in a
napkin to hide in my red cape's pocket, for later, when
I stray from the story's path, join the wolves. For now,
we go back into what troubling dreams remain, knowing
we face uncertain endings, knowing that where we go from
here is another story, beginning.

THE BLACKOUT

On August 14, the lights go out, and
part-time conspiracy theorists invade
the streets like a reunion of opossum.
We'll have to throw all our meat out,
becomes the universal chorus of neighbours
who sniff air like loyal sled dogs left
to die in a hostile, unknown wild. The
kids don't care and play hockey with
owl-eyes already adjusted to the dark,
to the even darker shadows the puck's
shape makes as it scuttles the road,
slammed by the girl two doors down
after she won the faceoff. Someone yells,
Goal! and the street cheers for the
unknown scorer, the new smell of
meat searing, the polka-dotted night-sky.
Such a sudden sky like a black hole into
which any animal could fall. And, as a last
word on the matter, someone's snout points
into this blackness at the future when only
the Dollarama, lit like a factory, remains.

THE PSYCHIC'S VERDICT

Chalk-white bubble letters
on the sandwich board swear,
for just ten bucks, the truth
about eternal love and happiness
while the window's kid-smudge
blurs a burping lava lamp,
Buddha's belly and one dry-eyed
Virgin dog-eared from years in
the sun. The door beyond street-
light opens to carpet, gum-riddled
lines of abolished rules, boy spit,
as the proprietor's breath, hot
with fortune, competes over the
TV hawking cash for gold, passes
your verdict and, with hand
extended, awaits the terms.

THE MIDWAY

A woman outside the laundromat attempts opera,
holds a note too terrible to be real, her arms spread
like streaks of spilt Orange Crush. I step aside to avoid
her sticky embrace, falling instead into a summer that
lies open like a half-read book, where just yesterday
you and I cruised the midway which had kids coveting
other kids' prizes and alien heads transmitting respect
to Smurfs. Yesterday, you and I stood outside a gum-
smacking world of people buying illusion, the wind
trying hard to blow us over. We tasted the screams of
the defenceless riding Drop Zone, a needle of light in a
sky most never climb, and even the beers were sun-
stroked, and you laughed at the band covering "Video
Killed the Radio Star" badly, while enduring bloodless
glares from chain-smoking carnies. Yesterday, the
world pushed into us like an impatient crowd but only
you pushed back, as the wasps and I dived for cover
in abandoned tufts of cotton candy. Today, your silence
writes the air, suffocates me with its heat, while the
clouds charge like white flies, and the sun cuts the lake
into glittering slices I wish I could savour. Today, I fall
into a summer as slippery as Orange Crush reverb, as
open as that half-read book, but remember yesterday,
how the future sometimes stretched like a rubber band,
and threatened with its sting.

CONSUMED

Grey voices hover in the Toronto air I swallow;
your cigarette's ash like dandruff I brush off one
shoulder as we head to the subway. All I can
think about are cross-examinations, the questions
you never ask me. So I review the defence's attack
on the FBI analyst then, on the defendant's father,
and feel the air conditioning of the Orlando court-
house shiver inside my skin, try hard not
to squirm or complain. *In case you are*
wondering, I say, as we descend to the platform,
having already pointed out the father's belligerent
Yes's and *No*'s, *what makes a good defence*
witness, in this case, I pause for effect, *is a bad liar.*
Fifteen minutes later we emerge from Dundas
West Station, and it is easy, I explain, to fall into
the story, obsess over its inconsistencies, consume
its details. The smell of my anxiety's heat hits you,
and though you nod, you resume a previous discussion
on people's disregard for personal space. I edge
away, hear a GO train whistle as the attorney,
in my head, asks the witness an unintelligible
question. *Clarify your theory of defence,* drawls
the judge, hashes the Twitter feed, cries
every mother in America, as you say, *Just one*
more beer. I squint for staggering pulses of
light, and am glad HLN can stay focused, cannot
be distracted from duct tape analysis, the heart-
breaking heart-shaped sticker and its absent
function. The evidence is overwhelming, I confess
to you, *God, just look at those silent thirty-one days.*

But the street consumes my voice, and the story's
potential drowns in a streak of sirens, the juvenile
observations of other citizens. In my head, HLN
replays visuals of the day's big moments: mostly,
of the defendant, furious and talking behind one hand,
fearful that so long without a voice, her mouth has
disappeared; or the defendant checking for running
mascara, the vitreal floaters mutating into new,
unpredictable creatures to take over her eye. I bet
she looks at those black amoebas domesticating in
her retina as though she is the forensic expert, as
though she can find the microscopic proof of
her vision's efficacy, its truth; how it tells lies
to protect what it sees. All while the CSI on
the stand identifies the child's skull.

The Orlando sky teems now with lightning;
the courthouse grounds are dotted with spectators'
signs like scarecrows. Here, Toronto's real
estate teems with vacant apartment balconies; its
sky shelters a late afternoon sun desperate to
peer over a cloud's broad shoulder and singe
every open eye. All I can do is walk, my mouth
full and chasing arguments, or pass raccoons
talking to each other about the quality of the
city's refuse. You get smaller as you press forward,
escape the encroachment of consumption, my
potent miscalculation of your interest, and soon,
I reassure myself, I'll be home, gathering small
consolations to take away like evidence, listening
to the prosecution ask the faceless jury, *What do
guilty people do?*, waiting out the logical answer,
for justice to write the right ending to the story,

as sure as the defendant stares blindly past the
floating creatures poised to eat her truth's lies alive.

THE RED LIGHT DISTRICT

Oude Kerk's neon cross stabs the eye with tacky
white light, anoints the cobbled night-river blue. Voyeurs
caught in its strobe effects like a dancer's moves that
stop and start—all her blinding, confessional arms.

Koninklijk's bells ring as a bum communes with pigeons.
No distinguishing between all these flapping bodies: in a
window a boy imagines he is some kind of monster, while
three storeys above a redhead kneels, sateen shadowing her
devout, bobbing head. I intently

study light from Oude Kerk sainting each passerby (my
crossed, fishnetted leg rocking its foot in a red, spiked heel),
and survey my options, just as the boy's mother ruins
his near-perfect Frankenstein.

THERE ARE NO SOLID GOLD DANCERS ANYMORE

On Liberty Street it suddenly hits me: *There are no Solid Gold dancers anymore.* Then I get hassled for change outside the textile merchant's store I've been thrown out of for dropping ribbon spools and making a fine mess, *Thank you very much.*

I toss a quarter, start to walk and think, *Who can think of love when it's hard getting enough out of being alive?* Nature tries to cover me like velvet, make everything seem more romantic, but I gotta learn to ignore that shit.

Burned-out internet cafés, five-buck psychic, dollar-store music, and used condom swimming in puke: all within one block. I walk and think, how well we've put technology to work, *Thank God* that in the end, technology will save us all, make us all the goddamn same.

All I need is one late-night glass of habit and I'll be through, in just one year I'll be through with sweating red wine from my armpits, all my tense pores. Just one year, that's all it'll take and then I'll be through with this street, this town.

Red light. No cars coming, so who cares, I'm fucking walking, I'm like a hobo here anyways. What I do, what I've done, one day'll make a mighty fine epitaph: LIVED, LAUGHED, DIED. But maybe, in a hundred years, if you look up my name in a dictionary, no, Wikipedia, it'll be a colloquialism, have a definition, a lexicon, a history, just like Joe Miller.... Yeah, right.

I'm counting my time down as I walk one last time west on Liberty, picking at my cracked lip, my hands colder than when I was born. In my velvet-lined pocket is my opium for the audience—*Thank God* I always could make 'em laugh—oh, and sing a song as catchy as any Irving Berlin or Neil Diamond could compose:

I wanted to try
Oh how I wanted to say

To you so many things, like
That I think it's funny
That we wish on stars
That I think it's funny
How stupid we are
For wishing on stars and
How little it means
In the wider scope of things
And how better off it seems
To have only me
And my stupid little dreams

THE UNCLE WHO COULD WALK ON WATER

Half of the time we're gone, but we don't know where,
We don't know where
—Paul Simon

There. Can't you see? I'm smiling. My arm around
your shoulder. And you. All childlike in pink.

You don't know yet that I'll pull on the spaghetti
strap of your sundress, apologize like a madman

when you tell me to stop, that I'm hurting your sun
burn, your red red shoulder. You can't hear the grass

buzz, barbeque smoke, KISS in the background, but
I can, still. You don't remember how you felt after

you got mad at the game and rode off. *For good,*
you said to anyone, defiant at only five years old,

though we tried to stop you, your sisters laughing
at your anger. No one yet knew that visit was my last,

that I'd disappear trying to walk on water.

And no one knows how long it takes to find your
way back anywhere. How life is like that—

every day a little closer you come to making out your
own face like a police sketch, to seeing yourself clear.

But no one's supposed to see from where I am. And I
see many things: kids crossing forbidden bridges no

matter the season, or getting stuck behind wire fences,
their pink fingers poking at passersby, mouth-holes

gaping with words; and you, still that five-year-old kid
running into an ocean of meaningless words, still

on the lookout for the right ones to say what you mean.
What you meant to say.

There you are—
Here I am—

Half of the time you don't know where—one arm
still hanging off that red red shoulder.

THE SWINE AND THE PEARL

After Jeanne Hébuterne

You are in this room, sickening.
Sardine heads mock our hunger, laugh
their oily eyes out.

I hold nothing and every one of your arms,
like you are an octopus but with only
one good hand.

The days grow tired, no one comes. As
though the city died, not us.

You are not the fortune-teller Apollinaire
posited that first time in La Rotonde, where
I had come to know other poor prophets,

their part-time allegiance to art's next Jesus.
No. You tell no future. Instead, you are horrible,
and smell. You are glorious,

and modern. You make me this too, and I am
yours for that. My face is your hand, your hand
against my face. It is meaningless, pain.

It is meaningless, dying.

You know no other form; I see this now.
I could be better than you. My hand could grow,
past yours.

I could be a name on future's lip.

HEADS OR TAILS

Leftover Doritos and Twizzler wrappers
archive this trip, our crumb-upholstered
dissonance. When the LTD cuts you off,
you accelerate, welcome the distraction,
the spite of two indignant engines, a promise
to redecorate the road with hubcaps. I chew
on corroded breath, the words, *D'ya trust me?*,
as you smirk, flip your eyes like a coin toss
I fear to call; and after your retinas steady,
the archival debris of our time together purls,
and one overturned car gleams like nickel.

THE SMALL PART OF THE UNIVERSE

The streetcar passes Jim's Restaurant, a place
someone once said we should go, that still
boasts *the best westerns,* and the rails squeal
with the universal truths of girls, *You know*
me!, as they gawk at one another's shoes. I
look to my right, but no one is there, and how
to know anyone in a world of half-light, where
girls speak so boldly to shadows, and I have no
words, only eyes to see couples relacing one
another's heart, or dodging the Seaton Street
playground that slides misfit teens in and out
of no one's arms. Years ago, this was a new city,
and everywhere I went, books pointed out the
theological implications of well-mapped streets,
the logic of direction, the journey to the church
door, while I carried broken Roman statuary in
my purse in case of an emergency, in case I had
to leave a trail. (The poetics of that fear remain
embedded in the cracked leather.) Then, I thought
myself so smart, able to rise to art's challenge
with my newly learned theories and acquired
expertise to fix the hole on Bathurst Street that
was my small part of the universe. Yes, I thought
myself so smart; me, reconstructing other artists's
intentions, and you, that someone who lay out
blueprints, stencilled in expert hand an imagined
city. You wanted to write its stone face, and wide,
unbarricaded streets, into a new language of
impeccable function. But in this imagined city,
cold with mirrors north on University Avenue,

I did not know how I should live, how you saw
me reflecting in your plans, only how I saw myself:
the Winged Victory atop the Princes' Gate, her
wingspan a glowing appraisal of jewelled white,
her feet poised to take flight off a gilded stylobate,
her drapery a perfect windswept Hellenistic sign.
And that image still jostles in my purse, a loud
remembrance, as I pass the ghost of Thrift Town,
a place we used to go, a place that dangled old
wedding dresses like legs off an iron railing, that
bragged with the pulse of glamorous disaster. And,
if I turn to look back at the design of years, of
the streets we knew like orthogonal grids, tender
as nerve endings, I might lose direction and
find you written everywhere, like the driver who
announces *Sorauren* as if he has found a princess
waiting for her ride into midnight. Like her, I
have left and been left with midnight, a once-
imagined city, once-imagined life, back when
I cut the night air with my wings. And that
fairytale never translated, remains undiscovered
amongst those now-packed books. So I turn
to the streetcar girls, but they are long gone,
have rejected midnight, are busy replanning
the city's urban structure, armature and posture,
their lovely pink heels inventing new steps into
the future, toes pointed to the sublime, surging
ahead, arriving, almost there.

MAGNIFICENT THINGS SURELY WILL COME

This summer, streets reek of defiant glamour, and hot-
pink fingernails like talons scratch the air. I play Shirley
Bassey for the strangers who slither in with sangria and
stories no one should hear, and endure the cruise of
chemical Kit Kat clouding Sterling Avenue, my conscience.
This summer, you kill yourself while I job search,
wander Walmart's maze of aisles, the devastating weight
of stuff; and George Noory talks, each night, to a guy
about the Antichrist, and men, each morning, navigate
the slippery pink roof of another new condo complex.
This summer, mourners manoeuvre conversation that
flutters then darts away, and vases of professionally arranged
daisies and chrysanthemums stand at attention, while
at the harbour, around the corner from the wake,
ducks, seagulls, swans and Canada geese frolic on
their private beach, mingle as easy as swingers at a party.
They joke about the kid who flings his kite at the sky, then
runs like hell. They guffaw at his father who picks up
the pieces, pulls at an invisible string, and runs too,
calling, *It's hard to get right the first time. But it'll be okay,*
because that is what a father has to believe.
This summer lies dangerous like exposed wire snaking
into a future where police cars burn, World Cup soccer
rages and *Teenage Dream* posters obstruct all Blockbuster
entrances. I watch the last chrysanthemum collapse,
each petal a single flower falling that I will never catch,
as women and men lean too far off the street's concrete
planters, their bodies begging for air, for water to quench
the grit's thirst, for this urgent lingering to go on, for the
magnificent things that surely will come.

NOTES

PART 1: *The Future Comes Anyway*

THE SEA-WITCH

The lyric "Ride your pony! Mony! Mony!" is from Billy Idol's "Mony Mony" (T. James, B. Gentry, R. Cordell & B. Bloom, 1968).

THE FAIREST OF THEM ALL

The lyric "to the total eclipse of my heart" is from Bonnie Tyler's "Total Eclipse of the Heart" (J. Steinman, 1983).

MATA HARI, CROSSING OVER

The epigraph is apocryphal.

THE AMAZING CRISWELL

"The Amazing Criswell" was inspired by the 1968 book, *Criswell Predicts: Your future from now to the year 2000!* by, of course, The Amazing Criswell.

The line "how could you make an end of our wicked beauty" is a riff on the famous line in the liquidation scene of *The Wizard of Oz,* as spoken by the Wicked Witch of the West (played by Margaret Hamilton): "who would have thought a good little girl like you could destroy my beautiful wickedness"; and the phrase "what a world" is from the same scene, and also belongs to the Wicked Witch of the West, with script by Noel Langley, Florence Ryerson and Edgar Allen Woolf (1939).

A MEMBER OF THE WAIT STAFF DELIVERS A GLASS OF ICE TO OPRAH

The line "the gathering of waters She called seas" is from Genesis, 1:10.

THE VOICE I WANT ONCE LIVED IN SAUSALITO

The title is inspired, in part, by *Creem* reviewer Stephen Demorest who, while reviewing Fleetwood Mac's 1976 album *Rumours,* had this to say about Stevie Nicks: "...there's only one cut that really sends me—'Dreams' written by Stevie Nicks. Look, I know she has an air that she's hot stuff, and it broke my heart too when she frosted her hair like someone's pet Yorkie last year, but when I get around to assembling my bionic playmate, that's the voice I want—lazily sensual, with a glassy baby shiver that can melt your heart faster than Bain de Soleil sliding down a greased thigh at the Beverly Hills Hotel pool."

The lyric "the edge of seventeen" is from Stevie Nicks' "Edge of Seventeen" (S. Nicks, 1981).

The line "it is all happening" belongs to the one and only Rodney Bingenheimer.

THE FUTURE COMES ANYWAY

The title is a line from Rainer Maria Rilke's *Letters to a Young Poet.*

The opening line, "We blink, and it is years, not hours later," is inspired by poet Pete Winslow's line, "I blink and half my life is over."

The phrase "little cruelty" comes from stage directions in Arthur Miller's *Death of a Salesman.*

PART 2: *Production 1060*

EPIGRAPHS

"People ask me, 'it must have been fun, making that picture…' Fun? Like hell it was fun! It was a lot of hard work" is from Jack Haley's memoir, *Heart of the Tin Man,* R.J. Communications, 1978, page 178.

"…In the case of a beloved film, *we are all the stars' doubles….* We are the stand-ins now" is from Salman Rushdie's *The Wizard of Oz,* BFI, 1992, page 46.

THE TIN MAN'S TAKE ON THE HEART

The poem takes its inspiration, in part, from Jack Haley's memoir.

Vaudeville slang: "payin' yer dues"; "playin' to the haircuts"; "grand juries"; "handcuffed to the seats"; "second banana"; "top banana"; "to go big"; "take the veil"; "bang-up finish"; "soft-shoe shufflin". Sources: 1. Wayne Keyser's http://www.goodmagic.com/carny/vaud.htm; 2. Marian Spitzer's "The People of Vaudeville," in Charles W. Stein's *American Vaudeville as Seen by Its Contemporaries* (1984); 3. Frank Cullen's *Vaudeville Old & New: An Encyclopedia of Variety Performers in America* (2006). 4. Jack Haley's *Heart of the Tin Man.*

"the merry ol' land of Oz": lyric from song of the same name in *The Wizard of Oz,* by Harold Arlen and E.Y. Harburg (1939).

"Oh my!": dialogue as spoken by Dorothy in *The Wizard of Oz,* with script by Noel Langley, Florence Ryerson and Edgar Allen Woolf (1939).

"Joe Millers": To tell a "Joe Miller" means to tell an old-fashioned, corny joke. Source: Jim Holt's "PUNCH LINE: The History of Jokes And Those Who Collect Them," published in *The New Yorker,* April 19, 2002.

THE GOOD WOMAN'S CHOICE

"animals worrying themselves into anemia" is a snippet of dialogue spoken by Auntie Em (played by Clara Blandick) in *The Wizard of Oz*'s opening sequence (known as the Kansas Prologue), with script by Noel Langley, Florence Ryerson and Edgar Allen Woolf (1939).

SURRENDER DOROTHY

The epigraph is transcribed from a 1967 interview Judy Garland gave to Barbara Walters, viewed on YouTube.

The poem re-imagines two moments in Garland's life: 1. The moment before she would go on live TV in 1955 for the Ford Star Jubilee to sing "Over the Rainbow" dressed as a tramp; and 2. Her much lauded debut at Carnegie Hall on April 23, 1961.

"Don't you know each cloud contains pennies from heaven…" lyric from "Pennies From Heaven" by Arthur Johnston and Johnny Burke (1936).

THE STRAW MAN

Biographical information on Ray Bolger from Frank Cullen's *Vaudeville Old & New: An Encyclopedia of Variety Performers in America* (2006).

Vaudeville slang: "chewing the scenery." Source: Wayne Keyser's http://www.goodmagic.com/carny/vaud.htm.

"I'm consultin' with the flowers… or is it the rain?"; "with all the thoughts I must be thinkin'"; the first quote is a deliberately misheard lyric, the second is correct, and both are from "If I Only Had a Brain" by Harold Arlen and E.Y. Harburg (1939).

THE MAN BEHIND THE CURTAIN

The story of Frank Morgan discovering he was wearing L. Frank Baum's jacket during a test shot for Professor Marvel is apocryphal, but does appear in Aljean Harmetz's 1977 book, *The Making of The Wizard of Oz*.

"at clouds that soon will roll me by" is a riff on the title of the song, "The Clouds Will Soon Roll By" by Billy Hill and Harry Woods (1932).

THE LION'S COURAGE

This piece owes a huge debt to John Lahr's fascinating and beautiful biography of his late father, *Notes on a Cowardly Lion*, from which the piece's epigraph is taken, as well as Lahr's December 30, 1956, appearance on *What's My Line?* in which he briefly addresses, with panel regular Bennett Cerf, his performance as Estragon in the North American premiere of *Waiting for Godot* from that same year.

Always Leave Them Laughing; "Everybody loves a clown"; "the joke ain't everything": title and lines from the 1949 film *Always Leave Them Laughing*, starring Lahr.

The following lines, scattered throughout the poem—"sing about love and happy times / About pretty things / About plucking strings / zayzoozas / How'm ah doin'?" are from Will Irwin's and Norman Zeno's "The Woof Song," performed by Lahr (though ultimately cut) from the 1937 film *Love and Hisses*.

The following lines, in the order in which they appear, are from Samuel Beckett's *Waiting for Godot* (1953): "to give the impression we exist"; "like leaves"; "All this lousy life I've crawled"; "there's no lack of void"; "Is that all there is? I'm going then"; "Shall we go?"; "We can't"; "Why not?"; "We're waiting for"; "I'm waiting for"; "come back to-morrow"; "And if they come?"

"subnoxious" is an example of Lahr's "ability to invent language" as referenced in John Lahr's *Notes on a Cowardly Lion*, page 174.

"have a little courage, that's all" is a line spoken by Zeke in the Kansas Prologue of *The Wizard of Oz*, with script by Noel Langley, Florence Ryerson and Edgar Allen Woolf (1939).

"gnong-gnong-gnong": Lahr's signature "sound," as discussed by John Lahr in the Preface to *Notes on a Cowardly Lion*, page xix.

PART 3: *The Small Part of the Universe*

THE UNCLE WHO COULD WALK ON WATER

The epigraph "Half of the time we're gone but we don't where, we don't where" and the line "Here I am" are from Simon & Garfunkel's "The Only Living Boy in New York" (P. Simon, 1970). The final line "Half of the time you don't where" is a riff on the epigraph.

CONSUMED

"Consumed" was inspired by the 2011 trial of Casey Anthony.

The line "my mouth full and chasing arguments" was inspired by the following lines in the Book of Job, 23:4a–4b: "I would set out my case before Him / And fill my mouth with arguments."

ACKNOWLEDGEMENTS

Some poems, in different forms, have appeared over the past sixteen years in *Acta Victoriana, Canadian Literature, Kiss Machine, Matrix, Room Magazine* and *Taddle Creek.* My thanks to all the editors. In particular, a huge and heartfelt thank you to Conan Tobias for years of unwavering support, his care with the poems and his good humour. Other poems, again in different forms, appeared in the chapbook *Gypsy* (Junction Books, 1999). The poems that comprise "Production 1060" were published in a chapbook titled *Production 1060: The Oz Monologues* by Junction Books in November, 2013. Many, many thanks to Carleton Wilson and Blaise Moritz.

Thank you to my dear friends who graciously read these poems and gave generously of their time and expertise when I needed it most. To Richard Almonte for his valuable edits and for always offering such sound advice. To Mary Crosbie for her most excellent suggestions and for always cheering me on. And, again, to Carleton Wilson for his extraordinary patience and superlative editorial work these past fifteen years—it has meant so much to me. I could never thank the three of you enough. But please know, this book is better because of all of you.

Thank you to Andy Boorman and Jiffy Pop! for so many things. Thank you to Julie Bot, Beth Bovaird, Jeanie Calleja, Gabriela Hahn, Paul Irving, Mary Milne, Sharon Moon, Sean Moore, Nushik Narsis and Moe Rosen for their encouragement and overall grooviness. Thank you to Sandra Kasturi for all the kind words. Thank you to Lynn Crosbie for years of support and inspiration. Thank you to Marjorie and Mike Boorman for all their support from so far away. And thank you, thank you, thank you, to my very understanding parents, Jacqueline and Ralph, and my sister Krista, for always being so awesome.

Thank you ever so much to Silas White and Nightwood Editions for taking this on. A huge thank you to the Ontario Arts Council and the Toronto Arts Council whose generous support assisted in the writing of this book. Finally, thank you to that psychic on Queen Street who started it all.

ABOUT THE AUTHOR

Adrienne Weiss is a college instructor and writer. She holds a BA in English from the University of Toronto and an MA in English from York University. Her first book of poems, titled *Awful Gestures,* was published in 2001 (Insomniac Press). From the late 1990s to mid-2000s, she was a member of the sketch comedy troupe the GTOs. She lives in Toronto.

A Junction Book

EDITOR
Carleton Wilson

TYPOGRAPHY & COVER DESIGN
Carleton Wilson

This book has been produced on 100% post-consumer recycled, ancient-forest-free paper, processed chlorine-free and printed with vegetable-based dyes.

Typeset in Adobe Arno Pro.

Printed and bound in Canada.

Junction Books
junctionbooks.ca

Nightwood Editions
www.nightwoodeditions.com